How People Lived

How People Lived in
Viking
Times

Colin Hynson

PowerKiDS
press.

New York

Published in 2009 by The Rosen Publishing Group Inc.
29 East 21st Street, New York, NY 10010

First Edition

Library of Congress Cataloging-in-Publication Data

Hynson, Colin.
    How people lived in Viking times / Colin Hynson. — 1st ed.
        p. cm. — (How people lived)
    Includes index.
    ISBN 978-1-4042-4434-4 (library binding)
    ISBN 978-1-4358-2624-3 (paperback)
    ISBN 978-1-4358-2638-0 (6-pack)
  1. Civilization, Viking—Juvenile literature. 2. Vikings—Juvenile literature. I. Title.
    DL66.H96 2009
    948'.022—dc22

                                        2007040218

Cover (main image): The Vikings were some of the first Europeans to play chess. This finely carved chess piece was made from a walrus tusk.

Picture acknowledgments: AKG-Images: 12; The British Museum London/AKG Images: front cover main, 25b; The British Museum London/HIP/Topfoto: 18, 23b; Martyn Chillmaid/PD: 19; Werner Forman Archive: 11; Richard T. Nowitz/Corbis: 16; Picturepoint/Topfoto: front cover cl, 8, 17, 21; Private Coll/Photo Heini Schneebeli/BAL: 13; Ted Spiegel/Image Works/Topfoto: 20; Statens Historiska Museet, Stockholm/AKG Images: 15; Statens Historiska Museet, Stockholm/Werner Forman Archive: front cover tl & bl, 3, 9, 26; Topfoto: 27; Viking Ship Museum Bygdoy/Werner Forman Archive: 7; Nik Wheeler/Corbis: 5, 10; York Archaeological Trust: 14, 22, 23t, 24, 25t.

Map by Peter Bull.

Manufactured in China

Contents

Words that appear in **bold**
can be found in the glossary
on page 28.

WHO WERE THE VIKINGS?

Between the eighth and the eleventh centuries, the Vikings from Sweden, Norway, and Denmark were one of the most dynamic and feared peoples in Europe. They sailed from their own countries in search of new lands to conquer and to settle. Their raids across Europe gave them a reputation as violent warriors. However, the Vikings also took part in trade with other countries. As traders, they traveled to places as far away as the Mediterranean and Asia, and even sailed to North America.

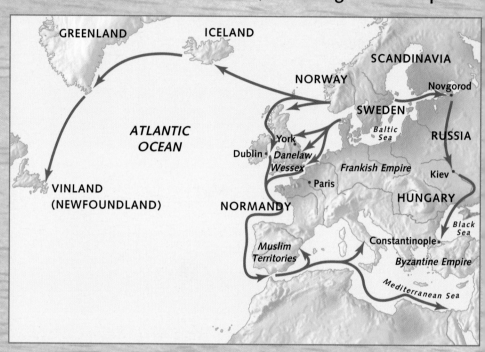

▲ This map shows how far Viking traders and settlers traveled across Europe, Asia, and North America.

VIKING RAIDERS

The fighting skill of the Vikings was legendary across Europe. Christian monks in England wrote in books and letters of merciless Viking raids on rich towns, churches, and monasteries. The attacks began in 793 A.D. with an assault on the English monastery of Lindisfarne. After that, the people of Britain, France, Germany, Spain, and Italy all felt the wrath of the Viking raiders.

VIKING SETTLERS

From the middle of the ninth century, the Vikings stopped their violent raids and began to settle peacefully in countries.

VIKING TIMELINE

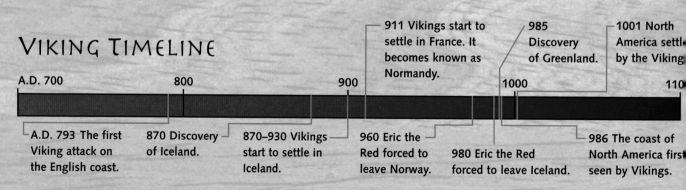

911 Vikings start to settle in France. It becomes known as Normandy.

985 Discovery of Greenland.

1001 North America settled by the Vikings

A.D. 700   800   900   1000   1100

A.D. 793 The first Viking attack on the English coast.

870 Discovery of Iceland.

870–930 Vikings start to settle in Iceland.

960 Eric the Red forced to leave Norway.

980 Eric the Red forced to leave Iceland.

986 The coast of North America first seen by Vikings.

Large numbers of Vikings moved to towns and villages in England, France, and Italy. Viking explorers found new lands. They discovered Iceland in 870 A.D. and Greenland in 985 A.D. In 1001, Leif the Lucky was the first European to set foot in America. When news reached home of these newly-discovered countries, many Vikings set off to start a new life. Between 870 and 930, about 10,000 Vikings left their homes for Iceland.

▲ This Viking boat was found at Oseberg in Norway. It dates from about 850 A.D. It was the kind of boat that would have been used by both Viking explorers and merchants.

A PICTURE OF THE VIKINGS

The Vikings gained a reputation for being a wild and uncivilized people. Although this is deserved in some ways, the Vikings were also skilled farmers, craftspeople, shipbuilders, and sailors. They created many fantastic tales called **sagas** and were skilled storytellers. They also ruled themselves much more democratically than was the case in many other places at that time by attending **things** (see pages 10–11).

REAL LIVES

ERIC THE RED AND LEIF THE LUCKY: VIKING EXPLORERS

Eric the Red was a tenth-century Norwegian chief who left his home after being accused of murder. He moved to Iceland but was banished after more accusations of murder. He then started to explore Greenland, and persuaded hundreds of Icelanders to move there. One of the ways in which he did this was to call it "Greenland," even though it is covered in ice and snow. His son, Leif the Lucky, discovered America.

VIKING MEN, WOMEN, AND CHILDREN

Viking men, women, and children were divided into three different groups or classes. The most powerful group was made up of the nobles, or **jarls**, who ruled over a small piece of land. Below them were the **freemen** who were landowners, farmers, warriors, and traders. Freemen were also entitled to take part in the running of their local communities. At the bottom of Viking society were the slaves. Slaves, who were usually owned by wealthy Vikings, did much of the hard work, both in the home and on the farm.

► This carving comes from Lindisfarne in northern England. It shows Viking warriors attacking Lindisfarne in 793 A.D.

VIKING MEN

Viking men, whether they were freemen or slaves, were expected to do most of the physical work, such as building boats. The Vikings also believed that men were supposed to protect and provide for their families. This did not just mean their wives and children, but also any other relatives who needed help or could no longer work.

VIKING WOMEN

Viking men were often away working as traders or warriors, so women had to take over many of their jobs back at home. Noble women ruled over their lands when their husbands were away. The wives of freemen ran their farms and households in the absence of their husbands. Female slaves carried out the household tasks in the homes of nobles.

VIKING CHILDREN

Childhood did not last long in the Viking age. The average life span of a Viking was about 40 years. The Vikings considered that children became adults at the age of 12. After that age, they were expected to behave like an adult, for example, by working or by getting married. Boys between the ages of 5 and 12 were often sent to live with another family. This was supposed to create strong bonds between different families. Viking girls stayed at home until their fathers found them a husband. Any children of slaves became slaves themselves as soon as they were old enough to work.

► This pendant shows a Viking woman welcoming a warrior who has returned home. She has long hair tied with a scarf and is wearing a long dress.

REAL LIVES

OLAF HARALDSSON: A CHILD VOYAGER

The Viking king, Olaf Haraldsson, is remembered as a warrior who converted to Christianity and then forced his subjects to become Christians, too. He started traveling at a very early age, joining his first raiding expedition when he was just 11. Within a few years, he was in charge of his own raiding parties.

WHO WAS IN CHARGE IN VIKING TIMES?

The Viking countries of Norway, Denmark, and Sweden were each ruled by a king. The kings had to be strong military leaders and they often took part in raids. They were also supposed to keep the peace at home and defend their lands from attack. Although these kings held a lot of power, ordinary Viking men and women did have some say in how their local areas were run. All freemen and women were allowed to take part in local assemblies called "things."

DUTIES OF THE KING

Apart from ruling their home country and taking part in raids, Viking kings had other duties. They represented their kingdoms abroad, and negotiated treaties with other Viking kingdoms and countries beyond. Kings also played an important role in religious ceremonies. Before the Vikings were converted to Christianity, kings had to lead the worship of their gods. It was believed that if they did not perform these tasks properly, the crops would fail.

▶ This modern statue is of Leif the Lucky, the son of Eric the Red (see page 7). Leif the Lucky was a great Viking chief who sailed to America.

THE JOB OF THE "THINGS"

At a local level, Viking communities were run by a "thing." "Things" were local assemblies that were called about once a year. Every Viking freeman was entitled to attend his local thing and to speak. The freemen discussed local matters, such as deciding on land disputes between neighbors. They also voted on new laws for their area, and even made decisions about punishments for lawbreakers.

WOMEN AND THE THINGS

Most of these local assemblies were made up of freemen alone. In some Viking lands, such as Iceland, women were allowed to attend their local things and to take part in any debates and discussions. However, none of the things permitted women to make any decisions or to have a vote.

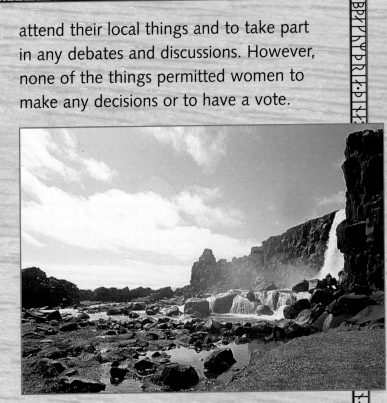

▲ The site of the Icelandic Althing. It is called the "Thingvellir," which means "Assembly Plain."

REAL LIVES

ARI THORGILSSON: A LEARNED HISTORIAN

One of the best-known things was in Iceland. It was called the Althing, and it met every two weeks in June and July between 930 and 1271 A.D. We know a lot about the Althing because of Ari Thorgilsson. He was an Icelandic historian who lived from 1067 to 1148. His most famous work was the *Book of Icelanders*. It detailed many of the debates that took place at the Althing.

WHAT WAS LIFE LIKE IN A VIKING FAMILY?

The Vikings took a great deal of pride in their families. Family "honor" was very important to every Viking. They were always loyal to another member of their family, even if they knew that person had done wrong. If one member of a family was injured or insulted, every member of that family was expected to seek revenge. This made marriage very important to the Vikings. Marriages helped to make a family stronger, and any children born made the family larger.

THE BRIDAL PRICE

Marriage partners were decided by the father of the family. When two fathers had agreed that their children were to marry, a bridal price had to be negotiated. This was a sum of money that was paid to the family of the daughter. The amount of money was based on how much it was thought she was worth. Her family also had to pay a dowry to the family of the son. The wedding date was set once these payments had been made.

◀ Swords such as this one were exchanged during the marriage ceremony. The sword taken by the wife was kept for her eldest son.

THE WEDDING CEREMONY

Viking marriages usually took place on a Friday. This was the day that **Freya**, the goddess of love and fertility, was worshipped, and it was believed that she could bless the couple with children. Weddings also usually took place in the summer. This allowed people to travel to the wedding more easily. At the end of the wedding service, the wife and husband drank **bridal ale**. This was usually mead, a mixture of beer and honey. After that, there was a week-long celebration of the marriage with feasting and drinking.

The same as in modern Christian marriages, rings like the gold ring pictured were also exchanged during the marriage ceremony.

AFTER A BIRTH

When a baby was born, it was shown to its father. He would then decide on what would happen next. If the baby was strong and healthy, he would return it to its mother. However, if the baby seemed weak or appeared to have a disability, the father would leave it exposed in the open air so that it would die.

REAL LIVES

A ROYAL MARRIAGE

In 1015–16, the Viking King Knut invaded England. When he reached the River Thames, he joined forces with his brother-in-law, Earl Eirik Hakonarson. An account called the *Lay of Eirik* describes how they fought together because they were related by marriage: "The noble marriage knot was nourished, I know, when king and earl entered upon warlike action."

VIKING HOUSES

Most Viking families lived in a single-roomed house. Viking houses were built from wood or **wattle and daub**, strips of wood that were covered in clay. Most houses were about 6 ½ x 16 ½ yards (6 x 15 meters) and were built to last about 30 years. Inside the house, there was a fireplace in the middle of the room. A small hole in the roof allowed the smoke out. Only the wealthiest Viking families had furniture, such as chairs or beds. Everybody else had raised platforms to sit and sleep on. There was very little privacy for Viking families, and everybody had to work, sleep, eat, and play together.

PREPARING FOOD

The fire in the middle of a Viking house was kept burning all day. It provided heat in the winter and was used to prepare all of the family's meals. Most Vikings lived close to the sea, so their most important and plentiful food was fish. The bones of cod, herring, and haddock have been found in Viking homes. Meat was cooked in a large cauldron that was hung over the fire. Preparing food was the job of the women in the family.

▼ This is a reconstruction of the inside of a Viking home. The open fire is in the middle of the room, and the women of the house are preparing a meal.

▼ This thirteenth-century chest from Sweden is typical of the kind of chest in which Viking families kept their valuables.

KEEPING THE VALUABLES SAFE

The women in a Viking household looked after the most valuable items in the house. In many Viking homes, this would be a large chest or box with an iron lock. The wife was in charge of the key to this chest. Many of these keys were beautifully decorated to show how important this job was.

CHILDREN AT HOME

Looking after children was the responsibility of the mother. Viking children were expected to behave very well at all times, especially when they were outside, or when there were guests in the house. This was because they had to keep up the family honor. Children also had to work inside the home. They helped with the cooking and cleaning, and even with running the family business, such as making sure that any slaves had jobs to do.

DID VIKING CHILDREN GO TO SCHOOL?

In Viking times, education was considered a luxury that very few could afford. Neither Viking boys nor girls went to school, even if their families were wealthy. One of the main reasons for this was that Viking children became adults at the age of 12. This meant that they had to learn about the work they would do from that age. Boys and girls simply learned from the adults they lived with. For boys, this involved learning how to fight and to have a trade. Girls were expected to learn from their mothers about how to run a household properly. However, there were some girls who learned a craft or even how to be a warrior.

▲ This picture is from the reconstructed Viking village of Norstead in Newfoundland. It shows a boy being taught the skills of boatbuilding.

THE EDUCATION OF BOYS

Until he was five, a Viking boy was cared for by his mother and other female members of the family, such as aunts and grandmothers. After the age of five, boys were sent away from home to live with another family. This was usually at an uncle's house or with somebody that the parents trusted. At his new home, the boy would learn all the skills he would need as an adult. He would be set to work on a farm and would also learn fighting skills.

THE EDUCATION OF GIRLS

Viking girls remained at home throughout their childhood. Running a Viking household was seen as a very important job, and girls were expected to know how to take charge of a home, particularly for the times when the men were away. Girls learned to cook for the whole family and to weave cloth to make clothes. Viking women often ran the farms when their husbands were away, and girls were taught how to take care of any animals that were kept by their families.

▲ This is a reconstruction of a Viking village in Denmark. Viking girls stayed at home in order to learn how to run a household.

REAL LIVES

FREYDIS EIRIKSDOTTIR: A VIKING WARRIOR

A few Viking girls were taught how to use a sword and become warriors. One of these was Freydís Eiríksdóttir, the daughter of the Viking king, Eric the Red. Freydís Eiríksdóttir led an expedition to Vinland in North America. Stories tell of her bravery in fighting Native Americans, but also of her cruelty. She beheaded some female prisoners that the Viking men refused to harm.

WHAT JOBS DID VIKING PEOPLE DO?

Most Vikings worked as farmers. The **Scandinavian** lands where the Vikings came from were mountainous and infertile, and the weather conditions were harsh. This made farming very difficult. It was the search for new farming land that led many Vikings to travel to Britain and France. Although Viking farmers did work hard, much of the most difficult labor was done by slaves. Women and children were also involved in farming, as well as having their own jobs to do in the house.

FARMING THE LAND

The Vikings had only picks and hoes to cultivate their fields, which made working the land even more difficult. They had to sow plants that did not need much soil to grow in and that could withstand cold weather. Their main cereal crops were barley and rye. The flour from these was used to make bread. Most Viking farms kept livestock, such as cattle and sheep. These animals provided food, such as milk and meat, as well as wool, which was used to make clothes.

▲ This board is made of whalebone and comes from Norway. It was used as a kind of ironing board. Women would use it to smooth their clothes.

THE WORK OF SLAVES

Slaves were usually captives taken after a Viking raid. Male slaves were known as **thralls**, and female slaves were called **ambatts**. Slaves were mostly used by wealthy Vikings, particularly the jarls, and they were the property of the people they worked for. That meant that slaves had no rights and no protection under Viking law. Female slaves worked in the home as a cook or cleaner. Male slaves worked on the farms, and were often used to put up large buildings and fortresses.

▼ This Viking loom was used to weave cloth. The warps, or upright threads, would hang from the top. The weft, or cross threads, would be passed in between the warps to make cloth. The large stones at the bottom made sure that the warps stayed tight.

WORK IN THE HOME

All Viking women spent part of their day spinning the wool that came from the sheep on their farms. The loom that they used to weave the cloth to make clothing for their family would have been propped up against a wall. Both boys and girls were taught to spin and weave, although only girls were expected to continue when they were adults.

WORKING ON LAND AND SEA

Although farming was the main job for most Vikings, it was not the only one. The Vikings were a great seafaring people, and they sailed far from home in search of places to settle or new trading opportunities. The Vikings traded with people all over Europe and as far away as the Middle East. They were also skilled at crafts such as metalwork and woodwork. They used many of the items they made at home, but traded with them, too.

◀ This carved head was found on a sled at the Oseberg burial site in Norway. The rich carvings show the skill of Viking woodworkers.

VIKING TRADERS

Trading was an important part of Viking life. This was usually done by bartering, since the Vikings did not use coins until late in the ninth century. Some of the most important items they traded were furs from animals such as deer and seals. They could also offer iron, wood, and ivory from walrus tusks. Through trading, they gained wheat and silver from Britain, wine and gold from the Mediterranean, and silk and spices from the Middle East. Goods from as far away as India have been found in Viking towns.

WORKING IN WOOD

The forests of Scandinavia provided the Vikings with plenty of wood for producing fine and intricate carvings. Some of the lands that the Vikings settled, such as Greenland, had few trees, so wood had to be brought over. Few of these wooden items have survived until today. However, in 1904, a burial mound was discovered at Oseberg in Norway. It contained the bodies of two women. An entire ship and many other wooden objects, such as a chest and a bed, were buried with them. All of these items were richly carved with complex patterns and human and animal figures.

WORKING WITH METAL

Iron was also plentiful in Viking lands and it was used for many different jobs, such as making tools and shipbuilding. Iron was used by craftsmen to make strong and elegant weapons, such as swords and spears. The gold and silver brought in by Viking traders was also used to make fine jewelry, including brooches and necklaces. Metalworking tools have been found in the graves of Viking women. This suggests that women were also involved in working with metal.

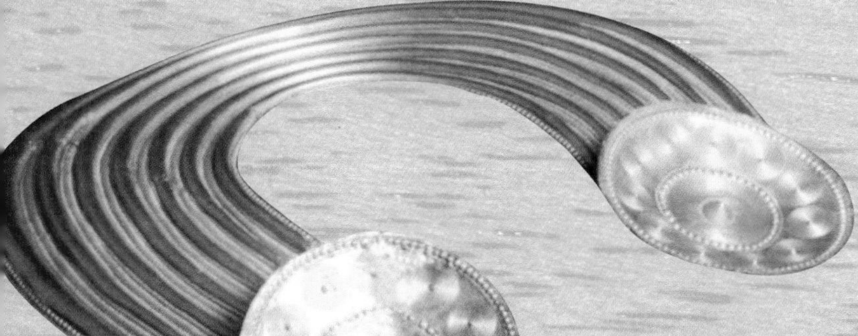

◄▲ Gold was very important to the Vikings as a source of family wealth. It was often turned into pieces of jewelry, like the pieces shown here.

REAL LIVES

IBN FADHLAN: TRADING WITH THE VIKINGS

In 922, an Arab trader named Ibn Fadhlan met some Vikings in Russia. He described the Viking traders he met as "the filthiest of God's creatures," although he also said that the Vikings were "tall as date palms, blond, and ruddy."

WHAT DID VIKING ADULTS AND CHILDREN WEAR?

The cold weather in Viking lands meant that the clothes people wore had to be warm and hardwearing. Wool and linen were the main fabrics used for clothes. Fine and delicate clothing had no place in the Viking wardrobe. However, clothes were still used to show the wearer's position in society. Wealthier Vikings found ways to decorate their clothes while still making sure that they were practical. Viking women indicated their status by wearing jewelry, particularly brooches. Boys and girls simply wore smaller versions of the clothes worn by their parents.

CLOTHING FOR BOYS AND MEN

In order to keep warm, both Viking boys and men always wore underwear. This was usually made of wool, which was probably very itchy. Wealthier Vikings could afford to have their underwear made of linen, which was softer on the skin. On top of their underwear, they wore a tunic and pants. Again, for wealthier Vikings, these were made of soft wool or linen. They would also have been able to afford a cloak and have fur added to

their clothes. Not only would this have kept them warm, it would also have shown their status in society. Viking shoes were made of leather and were slipper-shaped.

▶ These leather shoes and a knitted sock were found at Coppergate in the Viking town of Jorvik (modern York in England).

CLOTHING FOR GIRLS AND WOMEN

Clothing for Viking girls and women was made of several layers. The first layer was a kind of dress called a **chemise**. This was made of either wool or linen. It had long sleeves and went all the way down to the ankles. Over the top of the chemise, they wore a shorter overdress. This had shoulder straps and ended below the knee. In very cold weather, Viking women wore shawls. Married women usually wore a headdress or a scarf around their head. Shoes for women were the same as for men.

▲ Amber is a transparent pine resin. It was very popular with Vikings for jewelry-making because of its rich colors. The parts of this necklace are made from different pieces of amber.

WEARING BROOCHES

Vikings could show how wealthy they were by the type of brooch they wore to fasten their clothing together. Men wore small brooches or pins made of bronze or silver. Women wore pairs of **tortoise brooches**. These were oval brooches that fastened the dress at the shoulder. The brooches could be made of plain bronze, or highly decorated with pieces of gold and silver worked into them.

◄ This eleventh-century Viking brooch is in the shape of an animal wrapped in the tendrils of a plant. It would have had a pin on the back, so it could be pinned to a cloak.

HOW DID VIKING ADULTS AND CHILDREN HAVE FUN?

The Vikings enjoyed gathering together for feasts and entertainments. Huge feasts were often hosted by local nobles or jarls. A marriage, the successful return of a raiding party, or the end of a season all gave the Vikings a reason to eat, drink, and play together. At these celebrations, there was singing, dancing, storytelling, and wrestling matches. Vikings also enjoyed watching as horses were forced to fight each other. They placed bets on which horse would be the victor. Both men and women took part in the feasts. Children were sometimes taken along, too, but they were expected to entertain themselves with simple toys, and also to join in with some of the celebrations.

▲◄ These Viking musical instruments were found at Jorvik (modern York in England). There are some flutes made of bird bones and a set of wooden panpipes.

THE GREAT FEASTS

When the king invited guests to a celebration, it was known as the Great Feast. Kings often had a special servant called a **skald**. During the meal, the skald would entertain guests with songs and music played on a harp or on a flute made of bone. After the meal, the skald would tell stories about the adventures of the gods and recite poems praising the brave deeds of everybody present at the feast. These stories and poems were never written down and had to be learned by heart.

OUTDOOR ENTERTAINMENT

The cold winter days provided Vikings with plenty of opportunities to enjoy themselves. Vikings went skiing and used sleds. Ice skates were used by everybody. They were made from the leg bones of animals and were tied to the feet with leather straps.

▼ This picture shows how Vikings wore skates. A strip of leather would be threaded through the hole at the front of the bone skate and would then be tied to the boot.

INDOOR ENTERTAINMENT

Vikings enjoyed playing board games. The most popular game was **hneftafl**. This was a game in which one player used eight counters to protect a playing piece called the king from his opponent, who had 16 pieces. The game of chess arrived in Europe from the Arab world. It is believed that the Vikings were some of the first Europeans to play chess.

TOYS FOR CHILDREN

Children joined in with many of the games played by Viking adults. Carved wooden animals, particularly horses, were given to children. They also played with toys that were smaller versions of things used by adults, such as swords and spears. Toy boats and dolls made of wood have also been found at Viking sites.

◄ This finely carved chess piece was made from a walrus tusk. It was found on the Isle of Lewis in the Outer Hebrides, Scotland.

HOW IMPORTANT WAS RELIGION FOR THE VIKING PEOPLE?

The Vikings believed in many different gods and goddesses, who lived together in a place called **Asgard**. It was believed these gods could affect the everyday lives of ordinary people. The Vikings believed that warriors who had died bravely in battle would be taken to **Valhalla**, a great hall where they would join in great feasts every evening. By the end of the tenth century, the Vikings had been introduced to Christianity by missionaries, and within 100 years, the Vikings had become Christian.

VIKING GODS AND GODDESSES

The chief gods were **Odin**, **Thor**, and **Frey**. Odin was the god of wisdom and war. Thor was the god of thunder. Frey was the god of fertility. The Vikings also worshipped goddesses. Frey's wife was Freya, and she was the goddess of love and fertility (see page 13). **Hlin** was a goddess who cared for people who were mourning a death. **Nott** was goddess of the night.

▶ This Viking tombstone depicts gods such as Odin and Thor. It also shows a Viking warrior being brought to Valhalla.

Ship Burials

The Vikings had different ideas about what would happen when somebody died, but they all agreed that life continued after death. Most ordinary Vikings were buried in ship-shaped graves along with some of their possessions. Wealthy Vikings were buried in actual ships. These were filled with possessions and then either buried or set alight. The Vikings believed that by doing this, the dead person would be taken to the **next world**. The most famous ship burial was at Oseberg in Norway (see page 20). Of the two women buried with the ship, one was probably a queen and the other her servant.

▶ This Viking grave in Denmark is made of large stones that have been placed to make the shape of a Viking longship.

Reaching Valhalla

When a brave warrior died, the Vikings believed that his or her body was taken to Valhalla by the **Valkyries**. These were warrior women who decided which warriors would go with them to Valhalla. The belief was, that when the warriors reached Valhalla, they were greeted by Odin before being served food and drinks by the Valkyries.

REAL LIVES

THE FUNERAL OF A VIKING CHIEF

The Arab merchant, Ibn Fadhlan, witnessed the funeral of a Viking chief in 922. He wrote that the chief was "dressed in splendid garments ... Food and alcohol was placed next to the dead man, and two horses and two cows were cut into pieces with a sword and thrown into the ship."

Glossary

ambatt A female slave.

Asgard The home of the Viking gods and goddesses.

bridal ale A drink taken by a husband and wife during a marriage ceremony. It was usually beer sweetened with honey.

chemise An ankle-length dress with long sleeves, which was made of linen or wool.

freemen Vikings who were not slaves and were allowed to take part in things.

Frey The god of fertility.

Freya The goddess of love and fertility.

Hlin The goddess of mourning.

hneftafl A popular Viking board game.

jarl A Viking noble.

next world The place where the Vikings believed that people would go to after their death.

Nott Goddess of the Night.

Odin The god of wisdom and war.

sagas Stories of the gods and of brave Viking warriors. These stories were often told by skalds.

Scandinavia The Viking lands of Norway, Sweden, and Denmark.

skald A poet, storyteller, and musician employed by a Viking king to entertain his guests during a feast.

thing An assembly of Viking freemen and women that met to decide on local matters.

Thor The god of thunder.

thrall A male slave.

tortoise brooch An oval-shaped brooch worn by women to fasten their dresses and to show their wealth.

Valhalla The final resting place for Viking warriors who had died in battle.

Valkyries Warrior women who chose which Vikings would go to Valhalla.

wattle and daub The materials needed to make the walls of a Viking house. These were usually strips of wood that were covered with clay or even animal dung.

FURTHER INFORMATION

MORE BOOKS TO READ

Eyewonder History: Viking
(DK Children, 2007)

Christine Hatt
The Viking World
(Heinemann, 2004)

Susan Margeson
Eyewitness Books: Viking
(DK Children, 2000)

Jane Shuter
History Opens Windows: The Vikings
(Heinemann, 2002)

Philip Steele
Step Into: The Viking World
(Southwater, 2006)

Web Sites

Due to the changing nature of Internet links, PowerKids Press has developed an online list of Web Sites related to the subject of this book. This site is regularly updated. Please use this link to access this list:
www.powerkidslinks.com/hpl/viking

INDEX

Numbers in **bold** indicate pictures.